I Sh*t You Not
Little Teapot

Cera Wilson

BookLeaf
Publishing

India | USA | UK

Presentation by *BookLeaf Publishing*

Web: www.bookleafpub.com

E-mail: info@bookleafpub.com

ISBN: 9789358310207

First edition 2023

DEDICATION

To all of life's asteroids, forcing change, and
changing time.

Tullamore Dew

What is fresh dew if not the tears of the day
lived before
Soaked into the flesh of the earth
Creating new life
Recycled tears and fears
Some joy of course
But we grow more from pain
This is how we are created

In the morning as the day begins
Look and see the dew
Laid upon all you'll see
Give just a moment to those who created that
moment
Wish them a better day
And start anew
Remembering everyday starts with pain
Every morning starts with dew

Sitting in Cars with My Boy

Life hurls us forward
Life stops us dead in our tracks
Life is infamous for making little to all sense

We move so quickly reaching out as all things
pass us by
Grabbing through the windows of our souls'
moments
Moments that we may one day never know
again
We hurl through life, time and space
My only wish is that simply and forever May it
be I remember every inch of you and your
beautiful face

Air

Tongues slap against the air
No fear between here or there
Slowly you believe in what comes next
Afraid to want
Afraid to need
But yet here you are feeling somewhere in
between

A kiss
A touch
What is this new breath
As yours and mine begin to mold into one
I think, I hope you too feel this is more than just
for fun

Hands crash into skin
Slowly I understand where I end you begin

A kiss
A touch
What is this new sound
A pouring of you into me
All I hear taste and see

Circling breath

Breathe me in and I'll breathe you out
In this moment full of fear but no doubt

Love me once
Love me twice
Love me until there's simply only light

A kiss
A touch
What's this feeling
It's you
It's me
It's us

Double Field Yield

A pub
A glug
Cider with currant
Bringing some darkness within
That I can handle in this moment, not a whim
It would seem I finally feel more like me

Fill my cup and drink it up
A cider with currant
That'll do

A walk
A laugh
I haven't felt my feet move so fast
My mind so slow
I care not where we go

A sound
A dance
Play me a song that I suddenly hear a little
louder
I haven't heard a sound so clearly
My heart beats so slow
Is this what it means to be so carefree

A chat
A theory
My mind is racing with joy
Information no longer overloads
I forgot how smooth my mind does flow

Bring me my feet, my ears, my heart, my soul
For the first time in a while I now remember
how I glow

Inside and out
Here I am
A double yielding of the bee's knees
Hi there again love, it's me

Temporal Distortion

Through the looking glass of time
Stagnate
Untouched
We find time is of the essence
Yet time is irrelevant, unreal, and just a thought
A moment
Touched yet untouched
We are still and forever will be

You

Who am I to you
A series of moments
A series of people
A series of no one

Who am I to me
Everyone and no one
Someone and Star strung
Hanging lightly on a balance
Delicate but built like fire

Dancing between me and you
I see flashes of myself
But nevertheless I am not real
Just a being set free across space and time
Just being hurts sometimes
Just being hurts all the time

Who am I to you
Who am I to me
Faded lights
Shadows built somewhere between
the blacks and whites

Who am I to you

Who am I to me
If anything maybe the answer is
I'm simply unseen

Rush Rush

The sea tide grows
It begins its soft swoosh
It flows

The rain trickles along the walls
I'm reminded again that I can fall
Fall between the rising tides
For I am yours and you are mine

Roots

Roots tie us to one another
Grounded in a sea of memories
Ghosts stand upon a corner and wonder
Are we their legacy or is there still so much
more to be

The greens and golds form around us
I see a smile so familiar to me
Layers of people I've never seen

The world begins to slow down around us all
Time has a beginning but no end when night
begins its fall

A smile here
A smile there
I think in history all is fair
In love and war there is peace
It is us
Their legacy

Clank

Clank goes a glass to another
Yes that's true she is my Mother

Clank goes a glass
A smile so slowly passes
A smile between two strangers realizing there's
more to their story

Clank goes a glass
I can't believe they were so brass
Each as we are one generation to the next

Clank goes a glass
The sound of sweet memories
Drawing from the grapes and seeds
Dancing along smiling lips

Clank goes a glass
And time sits frozen in this short but sweet
moment

Don't

The questions flow like rapid fire
I can't keep this up
I am beyond tired

Don't ask me why I feel this way
My heart and mind sometimes delay
They walk together and sometimes apart
Move slowly with me please
I am only if in a moment just one piece

Don't tell me how I feel this way
I am not sure even what time passes in a day
Don't you see I'm two halves of a whole
One foot in front of the other seems too much
My heart and mind don't often know one
another

My heart and mind walk apart
And I know you feel lost
As have I
Since my very start

Be a bridge to my two halves
Use your steady hands to make each part
Walk in cadence and if you cannot

Then I simply ask you choose my heart
My mind may wander
It may make me lost
But I believe the compass lies right in my heart

Jangles of My Heart

Hang on your ladder
While holding my heart
Like a chandelier splatters
Twisted in parts

Vision of an open chest
Hand on the heart
Black tunnel upward
Reaching up With one hand
Pulling up the ladder
Towards the chandelier
With the other on an open rib caged heart

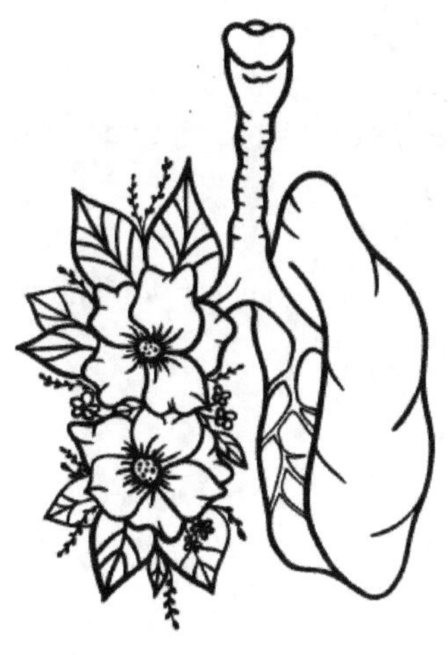

Dinosaur Piles

Passion can't conquer your fear of perfection
Did you know your eyes can't cash the checks
written upon your lips
Haven't you ever seen a single movie
Don't be the one who always ends up missing
me

Today
Tonight
Tomorrow
This doesn't simply just get better
Don't you see that I was made for you as you
were made for me

We were young once
Don't you remember how easy, moments never
felt like they were fleeting
Hours turned to tears
That's just the way this goes for you and me

Clear Water

Back down the road we go
Sounds whistle by like a train
We stop and we go

He plays his guitar
Maybe a banjo
Its however each note so chooses to flow

Winds blow and the light shines
Like a glimmer of a seaside town
I'll call you Pacey if you call me Joey
Let's grab a boat and leave this town

Back down the road we go
Sounds crash like the shores are made of stone
We stay and we go

He plays his harmonica
Maybe a tambourine
Its however each note so chooses to flow

Hold my hand and let's run awhile
Let the stars dance across my brow
As I look at you and into your starry eyes

Back down the road we go
Clear water is a back road
Where it goes only you and I know

Hold My Hand

The guitars rattle and a crowd sways
I reach over accidentally grazing your hand
You latch on quickly
And I think in that moment
Maybe you plan to never let go

I begin to sway and the music keeps going
Your hands feel so calm and steady
Is this what it feels like to be loved by you

The guitars begin to fade
Yet here we stand hand over hand
I look down and see you intertwined with me
The lights glow around our bond
Unbreakable yet I haven't even begun to realize
You'll be the one to always count me in

Jim Bond

Chamomile flowers
I know not what they look like
But I taste them each night

My nerves begin to fade and the day slowly
closes
I look around and see a home
The moment seems to last forever

I need this each day
Because closing my eyes I'm afraid
I want to feel
I want to touch
All of this again

Chamomile and heat
Pass through my lips
My dreams begin to brew
Hold me close
As I lay here and think of you

About A Girl

We locked eyes and I felt like you knew me
You asked me who you were
At first a beautiful face of course
But I knew you wanted to know more

We took a few steps and you showed your trust
You shared your fears and we worked to
understand each and every one

At first a pet seemed too much
Now a cuddle and deep sigh is how you greet
each night

Your eyes show wisdom
A wisecrack or two as well

I think you have lived by my side for many a
lifetime
Each passing day you grow and change
A journey we share
A bonded pair

Your ears move to the sound of my voice
And I know you hear me when I say
I love you Greta Girl

Thank you for showing me just how beautiful a
world this is

The Cinema

The sound begins the show
The nostalgia begins to creep in
A play on film what magic will we see

The butter glistens
The soda fizzes
Popcorn for breakfast says Grandma

A breathless smile comes across my face
These moments are timeless
They take place at anytime
Be clear not one of these moments is mindless

Art is on your screen
Get swept away
Be changed
Let the story take you anywhere

Think and reflect
Push back and argue
This is living art

Popcorn for breakfast she says
Memories for a lifetime
Moments on film

The reel spins
The show ends
But your story begins once again

Believe It

25

Sounds play in my mind
I take a step
It's a soundtrack in motion

This is what we call an adventure
Earth between your toes
Sun across your skin

Every step a new mission accomplished
Every sight a vision
Every moment a pause

Can you believe we live here
Can you believe this space is ours
Can you believe what your eyes see

Sounds play in my mind
I take a step
Poetry in motion

Just keep going
Everything you're looking for is just over there

Ripples

Water swells and begins to take shape
There is pain here
There is confusion

Water runs down in streams
Unhinged
There is truth here
There are only absolutes

Water dries against the surface
There is a release here
There is a realization

Water made its journey inside and then out
There is freedom here
There is revelation

Memoirs

Keep that memory for me
Hold it tight
I see it playing in your eyes

Looking through the webs of our minds
A compilation of Greats
A list and B list

What magic held between souls
We play memories we can't remember
With each smile and glance

Keep that memory for me
Hold me tight
I may not always be here
Except through your eyes

Bye Bye Love

I wave through breathless nostalgia
Sometimes hello
Sometimes goodbye

Each piece of this puzzle twists and turns
Searching for a partner and a place
Lay me here to rest

It's these moments I'm afraid I won't quite
remember
But these feelings
They will last forever

I wave through breathless realization
This time no hello
This time it is simply goodbye

www.ingramcontent.com/pod-product-compliance
Lightning Source LLC
LaVergne TN
LVHW010846200726
843508LV00012B/2777